THE
NIGHT BEFORE
CHRISTMAS

by Clement Clarke Moore
illustrated by John Steven Gurney

SCHOLASTIC INC.

New York   Toronto   London   Auckland   Sydney

A

PRESENT

FOR

GOOD

LITTLE BOYS

AND

GIRLS.

To my wife Kathie
for being a constant
source of inspiration

J.G.

Twas the night before Christmas,
when all through the house
Not a creature was stirring,
not even a mouse;

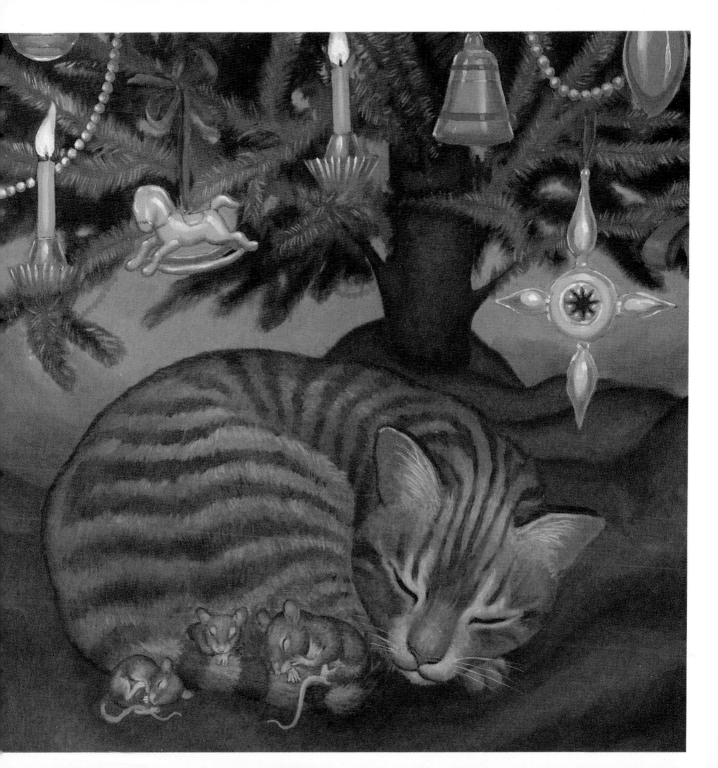

The stockings were hung
by the chimney with care,
In hopes that St. Nicholas
soon would be there;

The children were nestled
all snug in their beds,
While visions of sugarplums
danced in their heads;

And Mamma in her 'kerchief,
   and I in my cap,
Had just settled our brains
   for a long winter's nap;

When out on the lawn
   there arose such a clatter,
I sprang from my bed
   to see what was the matter.

Away to the window
   I flew like a flash,
Tore open the shutters
   and threw up the sash.

The moon on the breast
   of the new-fallen snow,
Gave the lustre of midday
   to objects below,

When, what to my wondering eyes
should appear,
But a miniature sleigh,
and eight tiny reindeer,

With a little old driver,
so lively and quick,
I knew in a moment
it must be St. Nick.

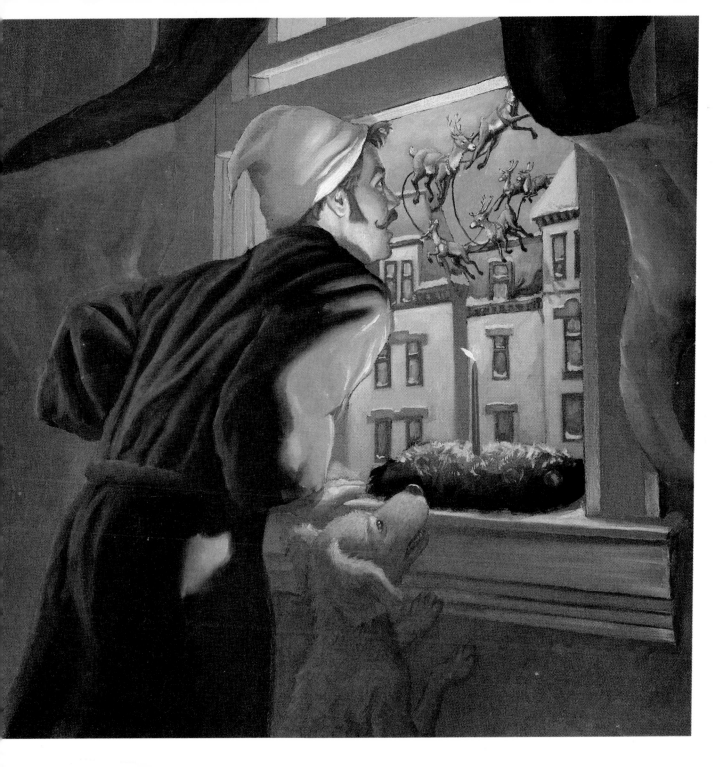

More rapid than eagles
his coursers they came,
And he whistled, and shouted,
and called them by name;

"Now *Dasher*! Now *Dancer*!
Now, *Prancer* and *Vixen*!
On, *Comet*! On, *Cupid*!
On, *Donder* and *Blitzen*!

To the top of the porch!
   To the top of the wall!
Now dash away! Dash away!
   Dash away all!''

As dry leaves that before
   the wild hurricane fly,
When they meet with an obstacle,
   mount to the sky;

So up to the housetop
   the coursers they flew,
With the sleigh full of toys,
   and St. Nicholas too.

And then in a twinkling,
   I heard on the roof,
The prancing and pawing
   of each little hoof—

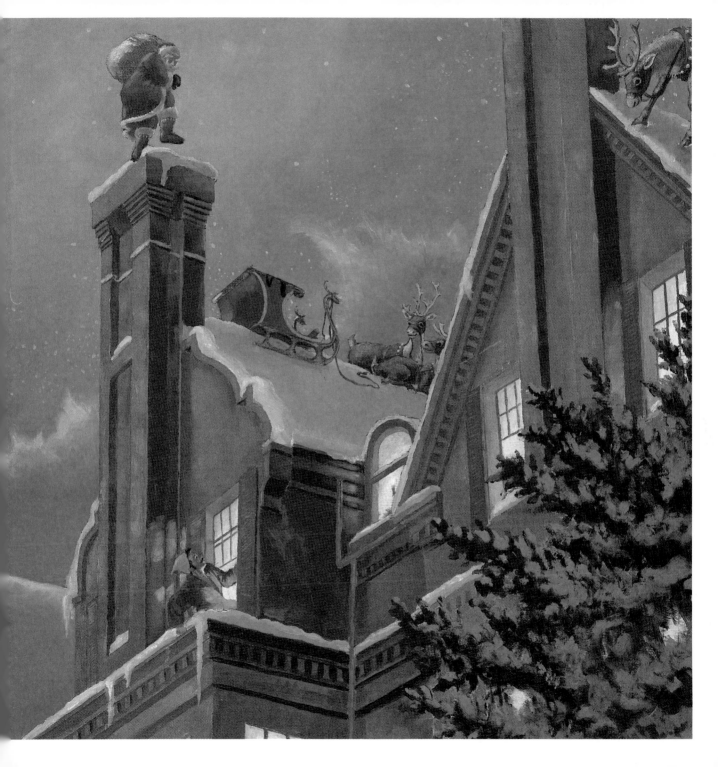

As I drew in my head,
   and was turning around,
Down the chimney St. Nicholas
   came with a bound.

He was dressed all in fur,
   from his head to his foot,
And his clothes were all tarnished
   with ashes and soot;

A bundle of toys
   he had flung on his back,
And he looked like a pedlar
   just opening his pack.

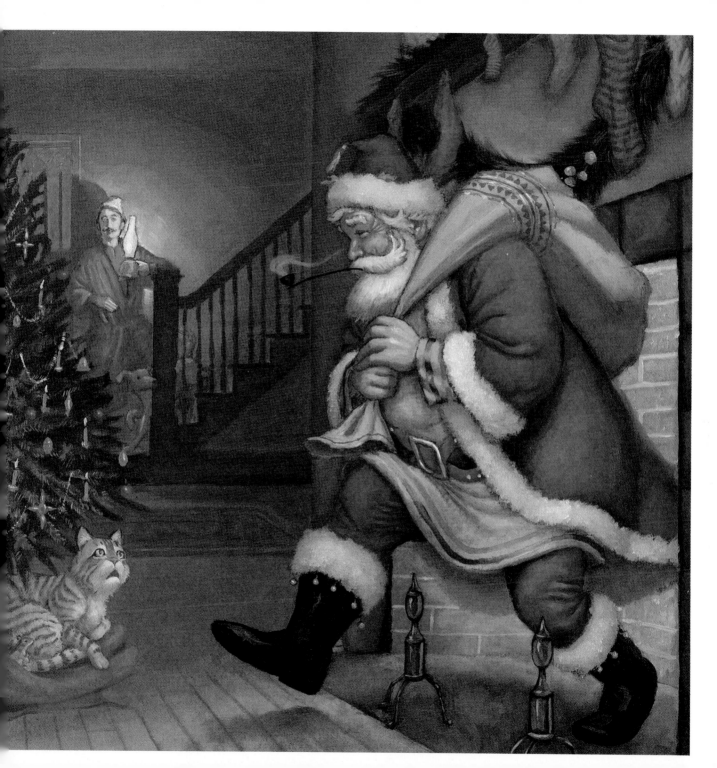

His eyes — how they twinkled!
   His dimples, how merry!
His cheeks were like roses,
   his nose like a cherry!

His droll little mouth
   was drawn up like a bow,
And the beard of his chin
   was as white as the snow;

The stump of a pipe
   he held tight in his teeth,
And the smoke it encircled
   his head like a wreath;

He had a broad face
    and a little round belly,
That shook when he laughed,
    like a bowlful of jelly.

He was chubby and plump,
    a right jolly old elf,
And I laughed when I saw him,
    in spite of myself,

A wink of his eye
    and a twist of his head,
Soon gave me to know
    I had nothing to dread;

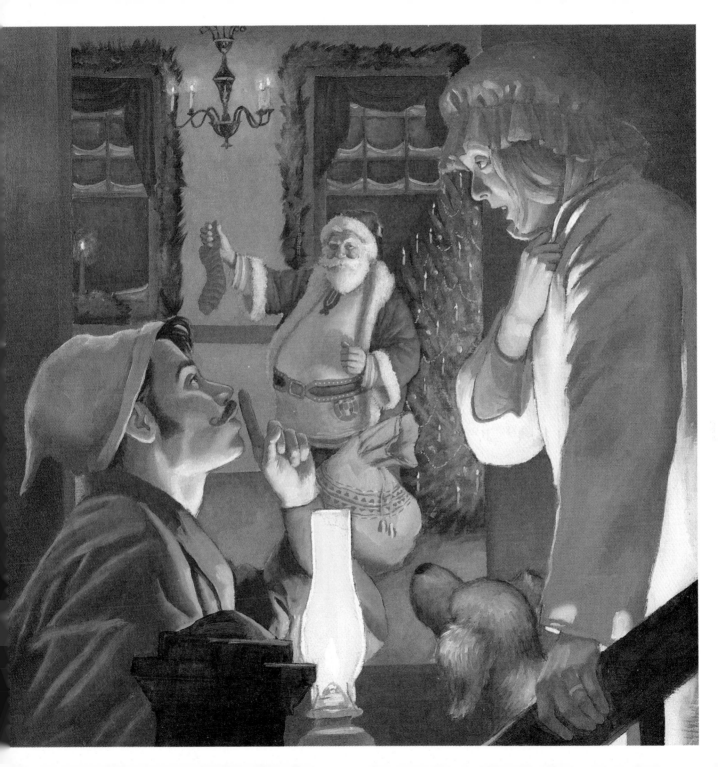

He spoke not a word,
  but went straight to his work,
And filled all the stockings;
  then turned with a jerk,

And laying his finger
  aside of his nose,
And giving a nod,
  up the chimney he rose;

He sprang to his sleigh,
   to his team gave a whistle,
And away they all flew
   like the down of a thistle.

But I heard him exclaim,
ere he drove out of sight,

"Happy Christmas to all.
And to all a good night."

ISBN 0-590-42758-X

Illustrations copyright © 1989 by John Gurney.
Designed by Theresa Fitzgerald and Joan Holub.
All rights reserved. Published by Scholastic Inc.

21 20   8 9/9

Printed in the U.S.A.   24
First Scholastic printing, October 1989